W9-ABU-031

DATE DUE

Look
After Yourself

Healthy Hair

Angela Royston

Heinemann Library
Chicago, Illinois

Designed by Dave Oakley
Photo research by Helen Reilly
Originated by Dot Gradations Ltd
Printed and bound in China by South China Printing Company

07 06 05 04 03
10 9 8 7 6 5 4 3 2 1

Library of Congress Cataloging-in-Publication Data
Royston, Angela.
  Healthy hair / Angela Royston.
      v. cm. -- (Look after yourself)
Includes bibliographical references and index.
Contents: Your body -- Your hair -- Take care of your hair --
Brushing and combing -- Neat and tidy -- Washing your hair --
Dry or oily hair? -- Protecting your hair -- Dry scalp -- Head lice
 -- Getting rid of head lice -- Getting things out of your hair - It's a fact.
ISBN 1-4034-4445-5 (libr. bdg.) -- ISBN 1-4034-4454-4 (pbk.)
 1. Hair--Care and hygiene--Juvenile literature. [1.
Hair--Care and hygiene.] I. Title.
  RL91.R883 2003
  646.7'24--dc21
                              2003000996

Acknowledgments
The author and publisher are grateful to the following for permission to reproduce copyright material:
Cover photograph by Bananastock.
pp. 4, 5, 6, 10, 11, 12, 16, 17, 21, 27 Trevor Clifford; p. 7 Powerstock; pp. 8, 15 Photodisc; p. 9 Pascal Crapet/Getty Images; p. 13 Angela Hampton/Bubbles; p. 14 Gareth Boden; p. 18 Nick Hanna/Bubbles; p. 19 David Madison/Getty Images; p. 20 Maria Taglienti/Getty Images; p. 22 BSIP PIR/Science Photo Library; p. 23 Lucy Tizard/Bubbles; p. 24 Martin Sookias; p. 25 Frans Rombout/Bubbles; p. 26 Jo Makin/Last Resort.

Special thanks to David Wright for his help in the preparation of this book.

Some words are shown in bold, **like this.** You can find out what they mean by looking in the glossary.

Contents

Your Body

Your body is made up of many different parts. Your skin and your hair are body parts. Each part works in a different way.

4

The skin on your head is called your **scalp.**
The hair on your head grows from **follicles**
in your scalp.

Your Hair

Hair helps keep your head warm. Hair also **protects** your **scalp** from the sun. There are many different kinds and colors of hair.

Some people have black hair. Others have red or blonde hair. Some people have curly hair. Others have straight or wavy hair.

Taking Care of Your Hair

You need to take care of your hair to keep it looking good. Keeping your hair clean is a part of keeping healthy. Clean hair feels better, too.

If you do not take care of your hair, it might get **tangled** and dirty. Your hair might get in your eyes. It might make your face feel itchy.

Brushing and Combing

Brush or comb your hair when you get up in the morning. Brushing and combing **untangles** your hair.

The wind can blow your hairs into knots and **tangles.** Brushing or combing them out can hurt. Hold the hair above the tangle before you comb it. This will keep it from hurting.

Neat and Tidy

Keep long hair tidy. You can use elastic bands to pull your hair back. You can **braid** your hair, too.

You should have your hair cut every few months. Cutting off the ends of your hair keeps it healthier and neater. Do not cut your own hair!

Washing Your Hair

Washing your hair cleans your **scalp** and your hair. It helps to keep your scalp from getting itchy. You need to wash your hair with **shampoo** at least once a week.

Make sure you rinse out all the shampoo when you have washed your hair. If you do not, your hair will feel sticky and will soon get dirty again.

15

Dry or Oily Hair?

Your **scalp** makes **natural oil.** The oil keeps your hair shiny. Some people have more natural oil than others. Use a **shampoo** that suits your hair.

moisture soak

Hydrates
and moisturises
dry/damaged hair

300 ml 10.1 fl oz

sheer vitality

Refreshes
and revives
normal hair

300 ml 10.1 fl oz

If your hair is very curly or dry, you can use a **conditioner.** Conditioner makes your hair more shiny and easy to comb. Some shampoos contain conditioner, too.

Protecting Your Hair

The sun can dry out your hair. Wearing a hat **protects** your hair. **Chemicals** in swimming pool water can also dry out your hair.

Wash your hair after you swim. This washes out the chemicals from the swimming pool water. A swimming cap can protect your hair, too.

Dry Scalp

The skin on your **scalp** may become dry and covered with small white flakes. These white flakes are called **dandruff.**

The white flakes are tiny pieces of dead skin from your scalp. You can use a special **shampoo** to get rid of the white flakes and make your scalp less dry. Make sure you wash all the shampoo from your hair.

Head Lice

If your head is very itchy, you may have **head lice.** Head lice are insects that spread easily from one person's hair to another person's hair.

Ask an adult to check your hair for **nits.**
Nits are the eggs of the head lice. They
look like small white flecks. You cannot
shake them out because they are attached
to the hair.

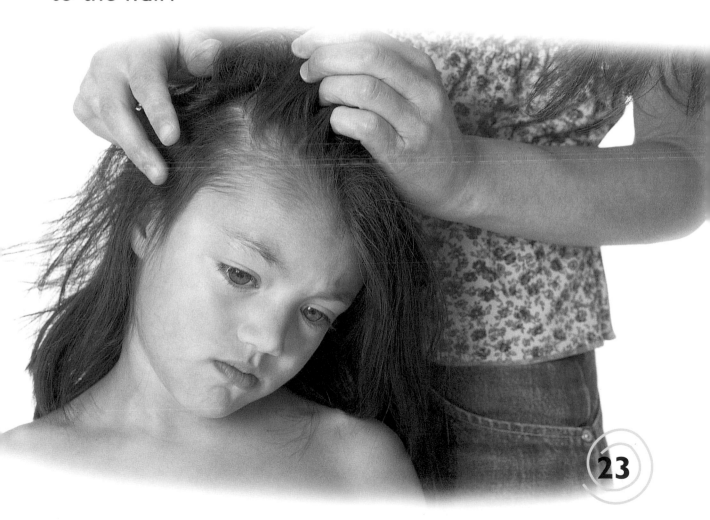

Getting Rid of Head Lice

You have to use a special **shampoo** to kill **head lice.** If you have head lice, tell your teacher. Everyone in your class and their families should use the shampoo, too.

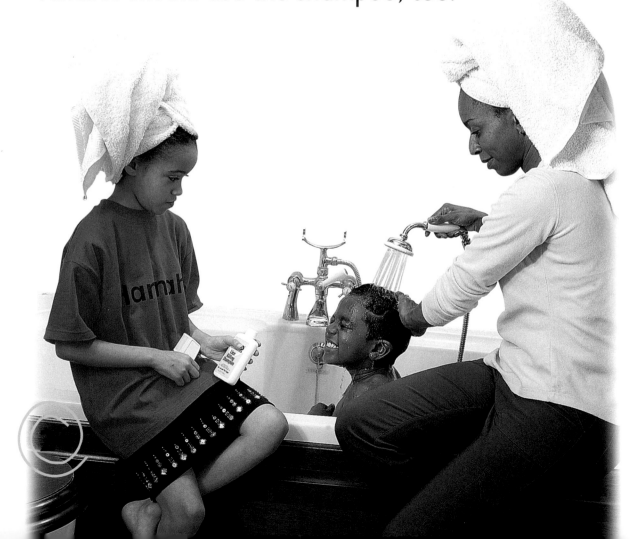

Once the lice are dead, you can comb them out with a special comb. The teeth of the comb are very close together, so the lice cannot slip through them.

Getting Things out of Your Hair

Sometimes things get stuck in your hair. Jam, honey, or ice cream can make your hair sticky. You have to wash your hair to get them out.

Some things cannot be washed out. If you get glue or chewing gum stuck in your hair, you will have to ask an adult to cut off that piece of hair.

It's a Fact!

About a hundred hairs on your head fall out every day, but do not worry—you have about 80,000 hairs on your head altogether. Brushing your hair helps to brush away the hairs that have already fallen out.

Children's hair grows faster than adults' hair. Adults' hair grows about a half an inch (about 1.5 cm) a month.

Each hair grows from a tiny pouch in your skin called a hair **follicle.** After a hair has fallen out, the follicle rests for a few months. Then a new hair begins to grow.

Each single hair grows for between two and six years before it falls out. This means that most people cannot grow their hair longer than about 31 inches (80 cm). Very few people can grow their hair to three feet long (one meter) and keep it healthy.

Your hair is not living. It is made of **protein.** Your hair and your fingernails are both made of different types of protein.

Some people have strong hair. Others have brittle hair. Brittle hair breaks off easily. Getting regular haircuts helps keep your hair strong and healthy.

Glossary

braid   to weave together three strands of hair

chemical   substance, for example, chlorine that is put into the water of swimming pools

conditioner   creamy liquid that makes hair less dry and more smooth and shiny

dandruff   crust that forms on the scalp and that comes off in small white flakes

follicle   small pouch in the skin from which a hair grows

head louse   (More than one are called lice.) small insect that lives in the hair and feeds on blood from the scalp

natural oil   greasy liquid made in your scalp that helps keep your hair shiny and healthy

nit   empty egg of head louse that is left behind when the louse has hatched

protect   to keep safe

30

protein chemical in food that helps your hair and your body grow

rinse to wash with clean water

scalp layer of skin that covers the top and back of the head and from which hair grows

shampoo soapy liquid that is used for washing hair

tangled twisted and knotted together

untangle make free from knots

More Books to Read

Noyed, Robert B. *Hair*. Milwaukee: Gareth Stevens, 2002.

Royston, Angela. *Clean and Healthy*. Chicago: Heinemann Library, 1999.

Vogel, Elizabeth. *Taking Care of My Hair*. New York: PowerKids Press, 2001.

Index

32